A Rose From Daddy

Written and Illustrated by Terry L. Nix

Published in the USA by
Terry Nix - Nature Art

Special thanks to my husband, Richard,
and my son and daughter-in-law, Mathew and Katie.
Greatly appreciate the time you took to help me with my project.

ISBN-13:978-1546391197
ISBN-10:1546391193

This book is dedicated to my grandchildren,
Rosie and Jonathan.
Jonathan has taught us great patience and
Rosie dearly loves flowers.

Winter Ends . . .

"What are you doing?" came the sweet voice of daddy's little girl.

He replied, "I am digging a hole in the soil to plant this bush."

The little girl giggled, "That's just a bunch of sticks in a plastic bag."

Her daddy smiled, "For now, yes, but after I plant the sticks, they grow leaves and pretty flowers."

The sticks in the bag are cuttings from rosebushes that grew last year. Her daddy purchased them from a local garden center.

The little girl ran outside, looked at the bush and exclaimed, "Where are the leaves and flowers?"

Her daddy looked up from watering and said, "The roots need to grow first under the soil."

"What are roots?"

"Part of the bush that stretches out underground to find food and water to help it grow."

If her daddy could show his little girl
under the soil, what would she see?

She would see the roots spreading down
to anchor the bush under the ground.

Spring Begins . . .

"Daddy, something is on the bush," said the little girl pointing to the bush.

"Those are the leaves," answered her daddy.

"Where are the flowers?"

"You need to wait a while longer for the bush to grow more before it can make flowers."

The leaves of a rosebush have rough edges. There is usually a single top leaf and pairs of leaves going down a thin stem.

The little girl ran outside to look at the bush and exclaimed, "I see green leaves! Are those green flowers?"

Her daddy smiled, "Those are the buds that will open up into pretty flowers."

"What are those pointy parts on the sticks called?"

"Those are thorns and the sticks are called branches."

Buds are closed up when they first appear. In time, each bud will slowly open to reveal its pretty color.

Summer Comes . . .

"Oh, look, the flowers are so pretty!" said the little girl excitedly.

Her daddy knew what she would ask next, so he said, "This is called a rosebush and the flowers are roses."

"Will the roses always be the same color?"

"Yes, this rosebush will only grow this color roses, but not all rosebushes are the same."

Roses come in many colors. There are different types of rosebushes that grow such colors as white, red, pink, and yellow.

Her daddy walked into the little girl's bedroom holding a glass bowl and exclaimed, "I have a surprise for you!"

"Is this a rose for me?" asked the little girl.

"Yes, it is a rose to keep in your bedroom."

"It smells so pretty!"

Roses can be picked from the rosebush to bring into the house. They add a light scent to the room.

Autumn Arrives . . .

"Why are you cutting the branches?" asked the little girl.

"The time has come for the rosebush to rest," answered her daddy.

"It looks like sticks again."

"It will be fine. When spring comes the rosebush will grow again."

Every autumn the rosebush has to be trimmed so the roses will bloom large the following year. Her daddy had trimmed carefully to avoid the many thorns.

The roots rest underground during the winter. In spring they will be active and the rosebush will grow all over again.

The little girl ran up to her daddy holding a drawing and exclaimed, "I waited a long time to see those pretty roses grow, but they were worth it!"

"I am glad you are learning how to wait for things. That is called patience," her daddy said smiling.

The little girl smiled too, spun around in a circle, and stopped to give her daddy a big hug.

Ideas are Blooming . . .

Tucked in the dialogue of this book is a character lesson on patience. Read the story again and stop each place where the little girl expects something to happen quickly. Explain that patience means waiting calmly for something. Sometimes it may be a long wait. Share ideas on what activities can be done to make the waiting a little easier.

Read the story again and ask what comes next before turning the page. Fold up a large sheet of paper to create individual squares for drawing each event in the story. The squares can be cut out and scrambled up to be placed in order for sequencing the story.

Learn the parts of the rosebush and their function. Look up a part each day, draw a picture, and write a sentence on what was learned. Other parts not included in this story can be added to your lesson—such as petals and stems.

Look at the two pages about the roots . . .

1. Try this experiment to show how water goes through the plant. Place a flower in water with food coloring added, and mark the container at the water level. You can use daffodils or carnations. Try some with leaves too. Observe each day as the dye goes up inside the plant and the water level lowers. Explain how the plant drinks water through the stem like we drink from a straw.

2. Try this experiment to show roots forming and taking in water. Place a potato in a container of water, and mark the container at the water level. If the potato is too small or the jar opening is too large, use toothpicks to hold up the potato so the bottom half is in the water. Observe the roots forming, leaves growing, and water level lowering. Discover what forms first. Is it the leaves or the roots?

What are the tools found in the story?

How is each tool used?

Where does each tool appear in the story?

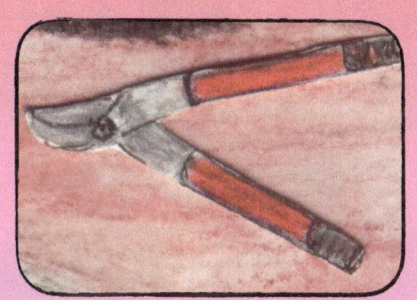

Take a trip to a garden center and find a rosebush in a bag or in a plastic container.
Enjoy planting and watching it grow!

Spring Begins Again . . .